Objects In The Mirror Are Closer Than They Appear

Saswati Sen

BookLeaf Publishing

India | USA | UK

Dedication

To the girl who fights stronger than Kali, Athena, or Oiá, loves and protects her own like an Amazon, and happens to be one of my best friends... Pallavi.

Preface

Life is the strangest ride one can be on! It is beautiful, terrifying, hilarious, heartbreaking, chaotic, thrilling, and full of random surprises waiting around the corner. It breaks us, builds us up, inspires us, scares us, is an exhilarating adventure one day but can become our worst nightmare in another. Still, it is a wonderful, wonderful feeling to be alive. The people we meet, the experiences we have, the aspirations, ambitions, failures, and loss all of it is part of life's never-ending charm. There are endless moments that we come across that demand some kind of response, and more often than not, we are too spellbound to speak. "Objects in the Mirror..." is a handful of occasional verses dedicated to such moments in life that require acknowledgment and are often forgotten in ecstasy or pain. They differ, in essence, from regular occasional verse, in the sense that they are not meant to be read aloud. They are same in spirit, though, and have been dedicated to moments, months, people, and occasions that have touched my soul. For much of the summer of 2025, poetry has been an escape for me from the roller coaster of emotions that life has taken me on. What balks or breaks me propels me to form them in words, and sometimes, sharing them is the only way I can leave room ahead of myself.

Acknowledgements

To Shohag & Argha, my rock and backup team forever, Maitreyi & Debasish, my parents, Subhadeep, Tanna, Reyansh & Mishka, my constant champions, Apoorva, my partner-in-crime and core member of my tribe, who keep me humble,(or at least try to). Thank you for the ways you make me feel supported and seen.

1. Remorse

Looking back after you leave, is deadly.
It is like choosing to go to a place where spiteful
creatures prowl,
ready to spring for your jugular.

It is like scratching old wounds,
till they turn raw and the blood appears in droplets of
habit,
reminding you of the pain.

Asking yourself what if you had stayed, is harakiri.
Question yourself and thence to the rabbit hole
where doubts, like rats, wait in silence.

It is like letting the flame too close to your skin.
The warmth soon begins to scorch,
and your peace burns down to ashes.

If you left, be gone.
Looking back is a wrong move.

Being on two boats never a good sailor doth make.
Move on and onward still,
let the past remain a milestone.

2. Objects in the mirror are closer than they appear

Of all the things we respect, time gets the last place.
We think we have time, a lifetime of it.
Ignorant of the fact,
that a life is measured in years,
and none of us know how many or however few we are
left with!
We argue and disagree, and speak our minds,
taking immense pride in the straightforwardness of it all.
No-nonsense, forthright and outspoken, are considered
compliments,
stamps of uprightness awarded to pretenseless citizens.
We pat our backs when we make no compromises.
Leave at the first flag of difference.
We believe there is always a next time,
unaware that this might be our last.
We wait for the right time,
that perfect twilight moment to confess our feelings,
that moonlight pier to ask for their hand,
when all along, objects in the mirror are closer than they

appear.
We sing and laugh and check our texts,
certain that it is enough to check the rearview mirror
once in a while.
So, we never see the crash until it shatters us,
leaving all our well-thought-out plans scattered like a
basket of toys in the backseat.
Of all the things we value, time gets the cheapest tag,
It gets back at us, sooner or later, often more than once,
leaving us with a misunderstood statutory warning!

3. Arroia

All she ever wanted was to never feel afraid as she
moved through the cobbled streets of life.
She longed to dance barefoot on sand, its grains rubbing
against her ankles like love!
She craved the taste of snowflakes on her tongue, as she
walked through the woods on a cold cold January
morning.
She dreamt of floating in the ocean,
drifting away in peace as the water caressed her bare
skin.
She yearned for the solitude of a remote mountain cabin.
She wished to savor a sunset by herself, far away from
the din and bustle of recognition.
She would walk in the moonlight and hear the wolves
howl, swim in a lake, in pouring rain,
pick fruits from an orchard, just her and the birds,
and feel no fear!
All she ever wanted was to get to know herself before
the world could teach her to fear who she could be.

4. Always

I want you to remember this,
even if you forget the rest...
that I will always love you.

We might not talk ever again,
but whenever it rains, know that I am missing you at
that moment.
When a pale blue harvest moon rises over the pumpkin
patch,
Know that I will be looking at it and remembering you,
wherever I might be.
When darkness melts into dawn, slowly like ice into
water,
at that hour
I would be waking up from dreams of you that pervade
my sleep, every time.

you may not see me ever again,
but each moment, each day
that takes me away from you farther into the abyss,

brings you closer to my heart.
know that I will hold on to your thoughts
like a dying woman holds on to the last twig she can find
before she drowns.

I want you to remember this,
even if you forget the rest....
that I will always love you.

5. Warning bells

How okay is it to be obvious?
How petty is it to be a cliche?
Does the one who lets her blues be hidden under
expensive concealer
turn green when her lover smiles kindly at a pretty
server?

Wealth and Content are step-sisters, I hear
They refuse to live under the same roof.
Guilt and Honesty are related by blood though,
they love to visit their mother, Penury.

Is it alright to be eccentric?
Is it acceptable to be plain?
Do people who lunch at Hamptons cry when a war-
ravaged orphan turns up on their social media?

Oblivion is the panacea for a long life, they say,
Ignorance though, is no longer a bliss.

If stones could talk,
Where would we flee for sanctuary?

6. June

And it's June once again.
The sky has started dressing up in brilliant shades of
pastels.
Crickets are back, and so are fireflies.
Parks everywhere are resonant with gleeful children.
Decks, balconies, and patios are once again favorite
haunts.
Twilights are heavy with the fragrance of roses, lilies,
lavender, and delphinium.
June brings back the promise of summer, of longer,
brighter days
and sudden showers that make everything glisten like
stardust.
The peevish bees, busy in the garden, going about the
business of making honey,
invoke life, again, in all its mayhem.

June is omniscient, it knows that summer won't be here
forever.
Still its dulcet tones promise that, while it lasts,

it would be magnificent!
June brings querencia, a sense of nostalgia for home,
a willing suspension of disbelief
that the endless summer days are here to stay.
Through hope, it wills us to forget that winter will creep
up on us eventually.

So, while June is here, with its rambunctious energy,
with its fairytales of golden summer days, lazy,
languishing warm nights under the moon,
let all worldly cares be forgotten, for a brief flash of
golden moments,
of living life on a sunshine whim.

7. No magic recipe

Thinking of all the moments that built up to this one.
The one in which seven thousand suns lit up my heart.
Sent it up in one big blaze
towards you.
Like a comet, like autumn leaves fleeing from an unseen
enchanter
I run
I run towards you.
Yesterday, today, and tomorrow.
I am not going to pretend like I couldn't help it.
It was no miracle, no quantum entanglement of souls.
It was a curious amalgam of moments, in which my
heart,
like a steadfast citizen, bore witness to the fact
that you are what I want.
And so I walked, towards you, in slow, sure steps,
until I started running.

8. Mokita

Have tornadoes heard about the Westerlies?
Are tsunamis taught about hurricanes?
Does lava know the power of avalanches?
Do dark corridors jump out of their skin, when they
mistake a shadow for a human?
I often wonder if our wolves know our demons!
Are they related by blood or dreams?

That blackbird that turns up on my balcony often,
I worry it knows too much about me!
It gives me pitiful glances, as if saying;" Oh you poor,
lost thing! Look at you all acting tough!"
My reclusive gray hairs have made quite a few new
friends,
They peek at my youth through the rearview mirror,
all sage and worldly-wise.

I keep thinking why deers are always in such a careless
hurry?
They never seem to be getting anywhere.

I worry if peace is an oft-told lie,
to keep us disruptors in check?

What if snakes came to know that their venom is
medicinal,
That they have been wrongfully treated for ages?
Did someone tell hugs they literally save lives,
do snaps realize they bring back hope?
What if one day we found out that we all could love each
other,
that these differences we fear are merely lores?

9. An apology to the person who asked me about my daughter

What do I tell you about her?
The girl who holds my heart in the palm of her hand;
The first time they brought her to me, her hair was more
golden than brown,
her eyes more blue than grey.
My heart left my body in that instant,
and has not returned to me ever since.

She is a math-magician, a girl of science.
She walks in the notorious lanes of Calculus with
fearless ease.
She talks about the stars and space,
unaware of the ones in her eyes.

Her French teacher calls her a Renaissance woman.
her father thinks she walks on air.
For me, there is no one but her,

I think that pretty much sums it up.

If you can keep your head around her,
you'll notice a heart that cares a lot.
For things that you did not know existed,
for causes beyond your radar.

You'll learn how Olms like to be wed,(an inside joke)
how penguins practice monogamy.
How Spinosoraus is her absolute favorite dinosaur
and why plastic is the monster of our times.

She is unlike anyone you'll perhaps meet.
No love for Harry Potter, no time for parties or dates.
She does not spend time in useless pursuits
problem-solving is her leisure interest.

She has the silliest laugh,
She blushes the same at a compliment or an unease.
She keeps on stumbling and bruising black and blue.
Insects terrify her, whether it's butterflies or bees.

Well, I hope I'm not making you weary
I should warn you that I can go on and on.
With myriad subtleties of her nature,
with endless anecdotes from her life so far.

You see, she just turned seventeen today.
It is my favorite day of the year.
I sincerely apologize if you hadn't seen it coming
but I'm only just getting started here!

10. No child's play

People speak of love as if it is a panacea,
a cure-all for all possible kinds of maladies.
As if it has the power to sprinkle magic dust on any
hapless soul
and turn all their woes into ecstasy.

Love is red in tooth and claw
It demands, takes, and then takes some more.
It brings out the worst in humans and renders them
useless for anything logical.
It draws blood, and knocks down the poor lovestruck
soul,
with moony eyes and quivering lips.

Love is ruthless,
without an ounce of mercy, at times.
It pounces on an unsuspecting victim, claiming their all.
So potent is its addiction,
that getting sober again is no easy task.

Still, people fall in love every day and rise.
Rise with the hope of wings
taking flight beyond tedium.
Love takes all but the power to disbelieve.
We are left to wonder if we were saved or ruined!

11. Give it your best shot

She is stuck some days.
Stuck beyond control
stuck so bad she can't breathe.
Stuck in the same routine
trying to break free
trying to fly and failing miserably
Her tongue stuck to the roof of her mouth.
Not able to form words.
She tries to flail her arms, but they are stuck too.
She struggles, fights, and then stops abruptly.
She knows what she wants.
She remembers the joy of unabiding things.
Of walking in the rain, shoes splattered with mud
straight shoulders, wild hair
droplets streaming through her face like love.
Heart dancing wildly all the way back home.
Now she breathes shallow,
The oxygen hoarse in her lungs.
Waiting for the wish to stop.

12. Côte d'Azur

Picturesque hamlets, lush green vineyards,
and all through the day, summer winds blow,
heavy with scents of lavender and frangipani.
The coastline is dazzling, azure,
the Mediterranean mesmerizes stupefies.
A chateau stands all by itself, amidst a deep foliage of
olive, pine, oak, and cypress,
away from the rest of the world.
There lives a woman named Céline.
No one knows her age.
Some say she is a young widow of twenty and five years.
some claim that she is about a hundred and forty years
old.
No one can vouch to have seen her.
People believe that the chateau is haunted.
Others say that the woman who lives in the house is a
witch.
No one dares to venture near.

Grief is a beautiful thing. Often useful,

it can make a woman more mysterious than she is.
Céline lives on undiscovered
in a house that was never hers.
No one knows about the rotten bones in the cellar,
Or the man who gave her a promise ring,
only to find out that he was unlucky in love
Everyone pities the young widow,
Unaware of the fact that she is neither young nor a
widow.
The ghosts in the house protest in unison.
They see everything. They know everything.
"Mon amour!" She whispers through a spiderweb of
wrinkles.
The stones shudder in response.
The ghosts cower in terror.
People believe that the chateau is haunted.
Some say that the woman who lives in the house is a
witch.
No one dares to venture near.

13. Un-Learesque

Ashes everywhere!
Piled high on the side of roads,
scattered on rooftops, painted on glass panes.
Who burnt memories in July?
And left the embers glowing until they turned into ashes
of the once-upon-a-time?
I can smell the remnants of the day,
you and I took a long walk.
The air smelt like rain-washed jasmine,
and you held my hand lest I trip on the cobblestones.
I dust off ashes from my lips,
but they taste savory like the roasted chickpeas we both
liked to munch on.

I look for a mask,
one of the numerous ones lying all over the house,
forgotten after a pandemic.
I need a shield to hide the subtitles on my face from your
listless ashen eyes.
There are ashes everywhere in your room, '

on your windowsill, in your bedclothes.
They smell like decay like life slowly ebbing away.
Like flesh melting off of bones.
There are ashes under my feet.
My skin smarts and itches.
What wouldn't I do to run as far away as I can from all of
this
to a blue, cold ocean!

I step out in the sun, hearing you call out my name, yet
again.
I don't look back in fear.
I hate to see you try to remember what you wanted to
say and fail.
As I walk, it rains ashes, as if a forest has caught fire
nearby.
I walk faster, desperate to get away,
but the cinders burn and burn and burn,
turning all the forty four years of my memories of you
into pale gray ashes.
I hear you calling my name again, and this time, I break
into a sprint,
through the fog of ashes,
away, away from you.

14. Joan-of-Arc

I need to speak the unspeakable.
I need to think the unthinkable.
I need to do the impossible.

Before the glass ceiling freezes to ice
Before hell takes over paradise.
Before the dead decide to rise.

Be warned! Hatred can often look like love.
Be wary! A noun can shapeshift into a verb.
Be alert! Landslides often start from above.

I want to be there before it starts.
I want to know how bad it hurts.
I want to save a few good hearts.

15. Οικία

I never went to see my house after they broke it down.
I turned my face to the other side whenever I passed by
Town Club this summer.
Town Club, the landmark of our house.
For years, we passed on the same information to friends,
guests, salesmen, delivery boys alike;
"It is the lane opposite Town Club. No, not the narrow
one, the one with dogs."
This summer, however, I refused to look at either.
It felt irresponsible, kind of foolish, that we let them
break down the house,
that stood for a hundred-something years.
It was coming apart at the seams though.
It rained more inside when it rained outside;
and the red cemented floor always felt wet these last few
years.
It had become an abode of my parents' discontent.
my mother's fears, my father's doubts.
In time it was destined to crumble,
its bones had turned rickety.

You could hear it groan at night.
It had become a sum total of possible disasters
when finally a young builder offered to buy it.
There was a collective sigh of relief.
And life went on its chosen way.
Two years later, when I went for a visit with my parents,
I heard that they had broken it down, taken it apart,
brick by single brick,
until nothing was left but the old rubber tree,
and the two stray dogs my father had adopted.
I spent the summer in distraught unease,
but never went back to see it.
Its demolition from the face of the earth seemed
embarrassing.
Sometimes we exist in a place that no longer is,
struggling to move forward from what was there before.
I still dream of the flowered bougainvillea over the main
gate.
Though I will never cross that threshold anymore.

16. Utopia

All those times we wonder "What if,"
look back again and again at the"Might bes,"
the "Could have beens,"
all our "Definitelys" wait, hurt, but patient,
hoping we will notice them.
We don't!
We mope and wallow for broken China,
which all the glue in the world won't fix.
Meanwhile, our "Infinities" fade away, unbeknownst,
forlorn, as we self-destruct into pointless misery.

What is it about us humans and "But suppose?"
Why are we so consumed by the "Almost?"
Why do we ignore the"Right in front of us" for the
"Maybe one day?"
We disregard time and tide in our delusion of
"Perfection."
We pursue possibilities over and over again,
never giving "Certainty" one chance at claiming our

souls!

17. Forever

I have known you for a million glorious suns!
In a thousand other lives,
In a hundred other forms.
Those hands that speak, I would know in a multitude of
people.
The smile that spreads like moonlight,
I have drunk from again and again.
Those lips have formed my name through centuries
alike.
I do not doubt that we will meet again,
I would know your laughter and your voice the same.
When we meet somewhere in a different infinity.

I do not fear death.
I will find my way back again and again.
Your soul is the North Star of my voyage.
Where beyond the realms of reason,
lies a magical land of hope.
I will travel time to find you there.
And I don't believe I am wrong

if I say I am you. You are me.
Never alone, always together,
like two orbs of light circling each other, for eternity and
thereafter!

18. Enkōmion

A sunset, A dawn, A moonlit street.
These are some of the things I would like to take with me
when I go.
When I close my eyes in the end, there should be a
phenomenal sunset happening.
Or a rain-storm would wash away all the dust,
Or an August moon should be rising silently,
where the ocean meets the horizon.

I would not rue or repent on what-ifs
I have had a magnificent life.
I have walked on grass, barefoot, dew drops, caressing
my feet.
I have loved like there was no tomorrow,
I have been loved and how!?
Like there was no one in the world but me!
I have tasted fruit, plucking them from the tree
and watched a summer day go by, syrupy and honeyed,
like a ripe peach.

I have carried a life to term, and given birth.
The miracle baptizing me forever into submission.
Tiny fingers curling around mine have sent my heart
racing like ninety-five on a fifty-five zone.
I have learned then that I have the ability to kill,
to wrench out a heart with my bare hands,
if anyone barely thought of hurting her.
I have watched my soul walk outside my body,
and I have lived, trembling and grateful.

Storm clouds! A silver moon! A crimson twilight!
These should be the things that remind people I have
been here.
I have lived life to the lees, drank it down to its dregs,
and danced in abandon, drunk with its boundless joy.
When I leave, I will take with me my daughter's laughter,
my lover's adoring whispers,
the love of a handful of good hearts.
And I will know, as I go, that I will come back
somewhere someday.

19. Nightmares

Strange things inhabit my dreams
Things beyond the realm of the known.
Veiled in moon dust, shimmering in darkness, minstrels
of the ephemeral.
They tiptoe in when sleep, like opium mist,
carries me Lethe-wards.
In that fog between consciousness and oblivion,
they stealthily enter, too pure for the waking eye,
gossamer denizens of my id.
They whisper impossibilities thoughts of love, mercy,
and hope.
They show me worlds where children are not bombed in
their sleep.
They show me a world where people live, laugh, and love
together,
black, brown white, or of any possible shade of color.
They promise me lies!

Morning comes soon enough,
bringing with it blessed reality, tearing through the

irrelevant hopes,
outrageous dreams!
I go forth into the usual chaos, living my normal.
"I need to talk to someone!" I mutter to myself, worried
about my sanity.
Strange things inhabit my dreams,
dreams that threaten to lure me to treacherous lands
where human beings seem to exist in love and peace,
free to dream, free to live!

20. Playing pretend

I have learned now,
to say "I'm good," with a big smile
when I'm screaming inside!
I have mastered the art of public relations in a social
setting,
air-kisses, side hugs, 'awwwww' ing in falsetto
and all the while my mind is playing in alto,
"Get the hell away from me."
I have graduated in appearances,
"Oh! I have missed this!" "We have to do it sometime
again, soon"
with people whose names I don't remember,
but pledge eternal friendship.
I have trained myself to indulge in
the slighter pleasure of running in circles,
when in reality, I would run away from all of this, a mile
a minute.
Life is the best tutor, it charges a lot,
but in the end, even hopeless students like me learn the
intended lesson.

21. Who said it would be easy

Who said it would be easy to be an adult?
Who knew that once you buy the subscription,
there's no going back and canceling it?
You might stumble and fall, get all bruised and battered,
but the show must go on, no matter what.
Your heart might break into a million pieces, but you still
have to pay tax.
Your brain may get fogged worse than an October
morning,
but you still have to decide what to eat.
Who do I call? You might wonder again and again,
There must be a way to get out of it.
But you'll find yourself alive despite it all
even though ten times a day your mind will scream, *I
quit! I quit!*
And then, on some days, you will give up the fight,
cause everything will suddenly seem better.
Fair warning! Those days will be few and far between,
but they will be there,

like wildflowers on a never-ending hike, breeze on a
sultry summer day,
and for a moment or two, you will think,
Well, isn't this nice?